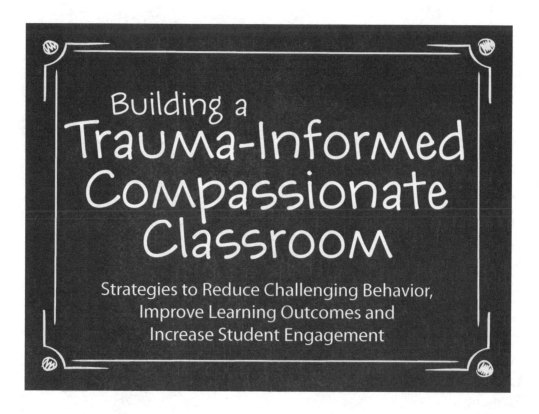

Building a
Trauma-Informed
Compassionate
Classroom

Strategies to Reduce Challenging Behavior,
Improve Learning Outcomes and
Increase Student Engagement

Jennifer L. Bashant, PhD

Copyright © 2020 by Jennifer L. Bashant

Published by
PESI Publishing & Media
PESI, Inc
3839 White Ave
Eau Claire, WI 54703

Cover Design: Amy Rubenzer
Layout: Bookmasters

Printed in the United States of America

ISBN: 9781683732754

PESI
Publishing
& Media
pesipublishing.com

Table of Contents

About the Author. v

Introduction vii

Part I
Understanding Trauma and Its Impact on Students

Chapter 1
Childhood Trauma Forms Cracks in the Foundation 3
  What Is an Emotional Foundation and Why Is It Important? 4
    Teacher Worksheet: Current Self-Regulation Strategies. 5
  What Causes Cracks in the Emotional Foundation? 6
    Teacher Worksheet: What are the Potential Effects of Three ACEs 7

Chapter 2
Withstanding the Elements During a Storm. 9
  Wired for Fear. 9
    Teacher Worksheet: What Stress Response(s) Does the Student Experience?. 11
    Student Worksheet: My Body's Response to Stress 14

Chapter 3
Rebuilding the Structure with New Tools, Skills, and Experiences 17
  Neuroplasticity 17
  The Importance of Developing Intrinsic Motivation 18
    Teacher Worksheet: Fostering Intrinsic Motivation 20
  Trauma-Compassionate Responses to Challenging Behavior. 21
    Teacher Worksheet: Crisis Plan 23

Part II
Compassionate Classrooms Are Conducive to Healing

Chapter 4
Building a Solid Structure with a Collaborative Classroom. 27
  Your Mindset Determines Your Response 27
  Collaborative Versus Punitive Discipline. 28
  Strengths-Based Versus Problem-Focused 28
    Student Worksheet: Mindful Communication 30
  Restorative Practices 31
    Teacher Worksheet: Today's Morning Meeting. 32
  What Does a Collaborative Classroom Look Like? 33
    Teacher Worksheet: Qualities of a Collaborative Classroom 34

Chapter 5
Connection Is the Cement That Builds Sturdy Walls 37
  Strategies for Forming a Positive Relationship 37
    Student Worksheet: My Favorite Teacher EVER 38
    Student Worksheet: Getting to Know You Survey 40
    Student Worksheet: Interest Survey... 42
    Teacher and *Student Worksheet: Relationship Plan* 46
  Connecting with the Family... 47
    Teacher Worksheet: Six Questions to Ask During Home Visits...................... 48
    Caregiver Worksheet: Home/School Collaboration Tool 49

Chapter 6
Triggers Are Windows to See Beyond the Behavior.......................... 51
    Teacher Worksheet: Identifying Triggers 52
    Teacher Worksheet: Trigger Inventory 53
    Teacher Worksheet: Improving Behavior by Planning for Triggers 55

Part III

Encouraging Personal Growth and a Positive Vision for the Future

Chapter 7
Resilience Is the Insurance Policy for Future Storms 59
  Showcase Gifts and Talents 59
    Teacher, Caregiver, or Student Worksheet: Neurodiversity Strengths 60
    Teacher Worksheet: Action Plan for Showcasing Strengths 67
  Teaching the Practice of Gratitude.. 68

Chapter 8
Instilling Hope Is the Promise of Unlimited Potential........................ 69
  Strategies for Instilling Hope 72

Chapter 9
Activities That Pave the Road to Success 77
    Student Worksheet: Noticing My Breath 78
    Student Activity: A Radical Act of Kindness 80
    Student Worksheet: Labeling Feelings 83
    Student Activity: Feeling Your Strong Feelings 84
    Student Activity: Compassion for Yourself 87
    Student Worksheet: My Personal Calming Strategies 89
  Empowerment Through Self-Soothing 90
    Student Worksheet: My Personal Mantras 91

Chapter 10
Final Thoughts 93

Recommended Resources 95
References.. 97

About the Author

Jennifer L. Bashant, Ph.D., LMSW, MA, founder of Building Better Futures LLC, is an educational consultant and motivational speaker, with the mission to provide educators with evidence-based strategies to reduce challenging behavior in the classroom and create a positive impact on learning. She is extremely passionate about her work, which is evident in her engaging, high-energy trainings and in her ability to connect with educators in a compassionate and authentic way. Her approach is trauma-sensitive and strengths-based, and she seeks to foster collaborative relationships between educators and students as they work together as partners in learning. Jennifer incorporates collaborative problem solving, restorative practices, and mindfulness in her work with students ages kindergarten through grade 12.

Jennifer is a certified trainer in DiSC Work and Communication Styles, EQ-i 2.0 Emotional Intelligence, mindfulness, and restorative practices. As a licensed social worker with over 20 years of experience, she shares her knowledge and expertise in a way that is heart-centered, practical, and relevant on the ground and in the trenches. *Building a Trauma-Compassionate Classroom* is Jennifer's first book.

Introduction

Educators in the United States are not trained psychologists, social workers, or counselors, yet they are often expected to serve in similar ways. Teacher training programs do not adequately prepare teachers for the demanding job of meeting the social and emotional needs of all students in their classrooms, yet there are students in every classroom who require a high level of behavioral support, and for whom "traditional approaches to discipline" do not work.

This book focuses on the specific needs of students for whom trauma has been a part of their lives. *Trauma,* **or an experience that overwhelms one's ability to cope, changes the wiring of the brain, and has an impact on both learning and behavior.** An incident or situation that is traumatic for one person may not be traumatic for another.

However, there are situations or experiences that often lead to trauma, including a home environment in which one is experiencing poverty; violence, substance abuse, or mental illness; having an incarcerated parent; witnessing violence in the community (or living with the fear of violence); and being the victim of bullying or of another crime. Every school and most every classroom has one or more students who have experienced trauma, and for whom trauma affects their daily lives. For this reason, it is imperative that educators have an understanding of:

- The behaviors associated with trauma and what they look like in the classroom

- How to create an emotionally safe environment for all students

- What is happening inside a child's brain and body when they are triggered, and how to respond to de-escalate the situation as quickly as possible

- How to help a student practice the skills to rewire their brain so it becomes easier and easier for them to self-regulate in adaptive ways

There are numerous books written by doctors and clinicians that define trauma and describe the negative effect on the brain, and all of these books serve a very important purpose. However, there is a gap in the literature in taking clinical knowledge and applying it to the classroom in a very practical way. As a clinical social worker, I will share with you my knowledge of evidence-based strategies for working with trauma in schools, presented in the form of very practical strategies and resources that you can incorporate throughout the busy school day.

It is one thing to understand the clinical manifestations of trauma, but it is another to know how to respond in the moment when disruptive behavior is derailing the lesson and affecting 20+ other students. As a school consultant, I have firsthand knowledge of the issues that teachers face, such as having a shortage of support staff and resources, very high-need students, and pressure to move very quickly through the curriculum. A teacher must know what to say (and what not to say) and do in order to keep all the children in the classroom safe.

Understandably, the teacher's response is often to send the student to the office for the principal to handle, but this is not the best way to manage the behavior because it does not get to the root of the problem. The end result is a vicious cycle of triggering events, disruptive behavior, being sent to the office, and back to the classroom again to repeat the cycle. **Without a clear understanding of why the disruptive behavior is occurring and how to effectively respond, this repetitive cycle is damaging to the student's self-esteem and self-efficacy.** Eventually, the student becomes disengaged in learning and begins heading down the wrong path in school and in life.

I became interested in understanding the effects of trauma as a result of an experience I had while I was in high school. During my junior year, another student brought a shotgun to school and ran through the hallways terrorizing the students and adults. The principal called for a lockdown and all teachers were asked to lock the doors to their classrooms. I happened to be coming back from the restroom and encountered the gunman, face-to-face, in the hallway. Luckily, he ran right past me and continued into the courtyard where the principal wrestled him for the gun and was able to keep everyone safe until the police arrived. After the incident was over, I can remember my body shaking from being in shock, and crying because I had been so afraid.

The trauma I experienced that day continued to affect me for about 10 years after. I was afraid to be alone, I always felt like someone was following me, and I had nightmares in which I relived the incident. Although this incident had a negative impact on my life, it also strengthened my ability to have extreme empathy for others who are struggling. I can easily connect with others and have a good sense about what they need and what to say to them.

The combination of my personal experience with trauma, the clinical knowledge I gained from my training as a social worker, and 10 years of training and embedded coaching with teachers in the classroom, all led to my passion for providing teachers with the tools to deal with trauma in the classroom. When not handled properly, challenging behavior can be the beginning of bullying, school violence, and even the school-to-prison pipeline.

When teachers are equipped to understand, prevent, and manage behaviors resulting from trauma, the potential for changing a child's life trajectory is great. **A meaningful connection to just one adult in school has the power to protect a child from many of the negative effects of trauma.** School connectedness in the context of a positive relationship is only possible in an environment in which a student feels safe, both physically and emotionally. Experiencing trauma does not need to lead to a lifetime of negative effects. With the proper knowledge and specific strategies, teachers have the tremendous opportunity to make a difference in the lives of their students every single day.

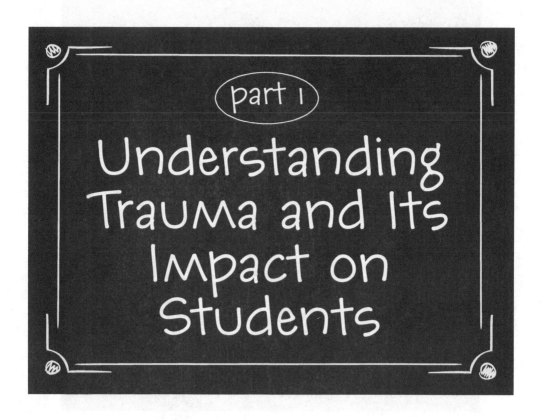

part 1

Understanding Trauma and Its Impact on Students

1.

Childhood Trauma Forms Cracks in the Foundation

As an educator, you are faced with much more than teaching your students the learning standards. In fact, for children who have experienced trauma or struggle with mental health challenges, it is futile to even attempt to teach the learning standards until the social-emotional needs of these (and all) students are met. This chapter will describe the components of a solid emotional foundation and its importance. Many of the students who walk through the door into your classroom have cracks in their emotional foundation, oftentimes due to having experienced one or more *adverse childhood experiences* (ACEs). The first step in building a trauma-compassionate classroom is to understand what constitutes trauma, and how it impacts brain development, and therefore, learning and behavior.

What Constitutes Trauma?

For the purposes of this book, **trauma is defined as an event or situation that exceeds one's ability to cope.** This definition is very individualized, which means that two people who experience the same event may not both view it as traumatic. Due to a variation in personality, social support, emotional well-being, and level of resilience, every individual has different strengths and resources upon which to draw. In other words, when trying to determine whether a student has experienced trauma, you must consider the degree to which the child was able to cope.

There are extreme circumstances that are almost certainly going to be traumatic for a child. Students living in poverty have inevitably experienced trauma when faced with food or housing insecurity, among other challenges. Students who have witnessed or experienced violence are likely to have been traumatized. Students who live in a home where there is drug or alcohol abuse are likely to experience trauma. However, students may experience trauma in less obvious ways, so it is important to view the situation through the eyes of the child, factoring in their ability to cope.

What Is an Emotional Foundation and Why Is It Important?

One of the important ways that children are able to cope with adversity is through the ability to self-regulate and self-soothe. Every human being is constantly seeking a state of emotional regulation. **When our emotions are regulated, we feel safe, calm, and content**. It feels uncomfortable to be nervous before an exam, fearful about failing, or overly excited while lying in bed at night and trying to fall asleep. Some people have been taught and are able to utilize adaptive strategies to cope with and reduce these uncomfortable emotions.

Adaptive strategies, such as meditation, exercise, or reading before bed, have a neutral or positive impact on the individual and/or those around them. Others innately turn to nonadaptive self-regulation strategies, or strategies that have a negative impact on oneself or others, which were discovered and learned through modeling or self-discovery. Examples of nonadaptive strategies are smoking, use of alcohol or drugs, and yelling at another person out of anger.

The first step in helping a student foster a healthy emotional foundation is to assess the student's current self-regulation strategies. The student's ability to implement adaptive strategies will impact coping skills, decision making, problem-solving abilities, and relationships with both peers and adults. What is this student doing to regulate their emotions and self-soothe?

Current Self-Regulation Strategies

This worksheet is designed to help you assess the type of self-regulation strategies that the student is currently using. After completing this assessment, the goal is to:

1. Closely examine any nonadaptive strategies that the student is using.
2. Determine the purpose that each strategy serves for the student.
3. Work collaboratively with the student to select an adaptive strategy to replace each nonadaptive strategy.
4. Explicitly teach each adaptive strategy and encourage their use.

Adaptive Strategies	Nonadaptive Strategies
☐ Taking deep breaths	☐ Running out of the classroom
☐ Listening to calming music	☐ Refusal or defiance
☐ Taking a walk	☐ Silliness
☐ Talking with a trusted adult	☐ Arguing and/or cursing
☐ Asking for help	☐ Physical aggression
☐ Exercise and/or heavy work	☐ Daydreaming
☐ Swinging/Rocking	☐ Avoidance and/or shutting down
☐	☐
☐	☐

Total: _____

Our plan is to replace _____

(nonadaptive strategies) with the following adaptive strategies: _____

_____

_____

What Causes Cracks in the Emotional Foundation?

Prior to 1990, it was well understood that health-risk behaviors, such as smoking, alcohol abuse, and sexual behaviors, put people at higher risk of developing disease and early death. It was also known that these health-risk behaviors were not evenly distributed among the population—certain people were more likely to exhibit these behaviors than others. But scientists did not know who these people were, nor did they fully understand the impact of these choices on their lives.

During the 1990s, the Centers for Disease Control and Prevention (CDC) began a large-scale study of over 22,000 people in the United States in order to better understand the people who were most likely to exhibit health-risk behaviors (Felitti et al., 1998). The study found that there are 10 factors that were significantly correlated with health-risk behaviors, and these factors are called ACEs.

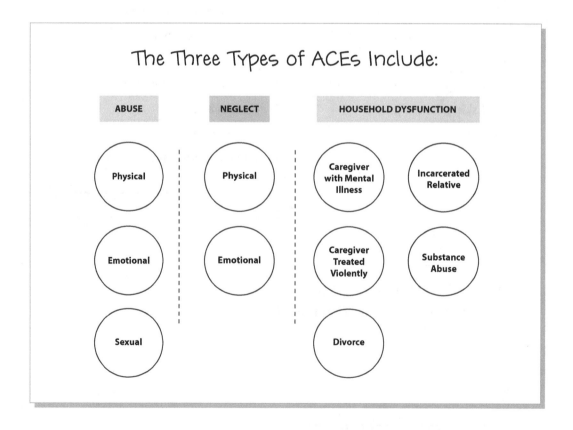

What Are the Potential Effects of Three ACEs in a Child's Life?

According to the CDC, the ACE study found that when compared with students with no ACEs, students with three or more ACEs are five times more likely to have attendance issues, six times more likely to have behavior problems, and three times more likely to experience academic failure (Felitti et al., 1998).

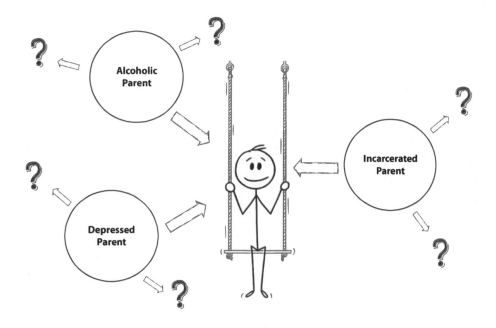

There are so many potential ways ACEs can impact a student's life. Imagine that the figure in the diagram represents one of your students who has three ACEs (an alcoholic parent who has depression and an incarcerated parent). Each one of these ACEs directly impacts the student's learning and/or behavior.

For each ACE, list two effects it may have on the child's life. After completing the chart on the next page, take some time to reflect on what it must feel like to be a child with three or more ACEs. The empathy that you will gain by doing this exercise will help you build trust and a positive relationship with the student.

ACE	Impact on Student's Learning	Impact on Student's Behavior
Alcoholic Parent		
Depressed Parent		
Incarcerated Parent		

2.

Withstanding the Elements During a Storm

As humans, we are faced with risk, danger, and sometimes harm throughout our lives. However, our brains and bodies are equipped with the capacity to help us survive threats and dangerous circumstances. The hippocampus is designed to take a snapshot of the environment and all of its components during a time of perceived danger. In other words, the hippocampus helps us remember what sounds, smells, and surroundings were present and makes an association with danger.

Wired for Fear

There are physiological changes that happen within the body in response to fear and stress. When we are stressed, the amygdala releases cortisol, and that cortisol, along with adrenaline, courses through the body in preparation for fight, flight, or freeze mode. We can trace this stress response back to the caveman days, where it was primarily responsible for keeping humans safe when faced with a dangerous situation.

For example, if a man was walking through the woods and suddenly encountered a bear, fear would cause cortisol and adrenaline to be released and the man would have a sudden surge of energy and strength to stay and fight the bear, or to take off running.

n a student is afraid, feels threatened, or otherwise does not feel safe, he brain and body set into motion this primitive, protective response. This biological response is essential when real danger is present; however, it becomes an issue when cortisol is constantly being released, even when there is no present danger. When a child experiences a prolonged state of chronic stress, this is referred to as *toxic stress*. Toxic stress leads to a continued release of cortisol. This leaves the child in an anxious, fearful state, ready to fight or flee at any given moment. Over time, this sustained stress response has very harmful effects on the body.

In order to help a student learn to manage emotions and self-regulate, it is helpful to closely examine how the student typically reacts to being triggered. The following worksheet will help you identify whether the reaction is most often a fight, flight or freeze response.

What Stress Response(s) Does the Student Experience?

Circle the behaviors that you notice the student exhibiting when they are responding to stress. Then, determine whether stress triggers a fight, flight, or freeze response in them.

Flight	Fight	Freeze
Withdrawal	Acting out	Numbness
Running out of the classroom	Aggression	Refusal to answer
Daydreaming	Refusal and defiance	Refusal to get needs met
Appearance of sleeping	Silliness	Giving a blank look
Avoidance of others	Hyperactivity	Inability to move or act
Hiding or wandering	Argumentative	Answering "I don't know"

The brain is always changing and adapting based on how it is being used, which is referred to as *neuroplasticity*. **When a student experiences toxic stress, the amygdala actually grows in size and becomes more and more ready to jump in and take over**. You may have had a student who seems to explode or become aggressive for no apparent reason, but what is actually happening is the student, in a constant state of hyperarousal, is triggered very easily. Anything can be a trigger, and because the student already has a high level of cortisol and a larger amygdala ready and waiting to take over, the challenging behavior occurs very quickly and very intensely.

When a student experiences fight, flight, or freeze in the classroom, it often goes unrecognized for what it truly is—a physiological response to a perceived threat. Recognition is the first step in helping the student. So how can you tell the difference between fight, flight, or freeze, and other challenging behavior such as oppositional defiance, hyperactivity, or avoidance? The following behaviors are the most common responses when a student has been triggered:

- Blowing up when corrected or not getting what they want

- Defiance

- Fighting—especially when criticized or teased

- Resisting transitions or change

- Unusually protective of personal space

- Reverting to younger behavior

- Frequently seeking attention

- Distrust of adults in authority

However, even physicians and psychiatrists can have difficulty determining whether the cause of the challenging behavior is due to ADHD or trauma. As an educator, you may or may not have information about the student's family circumstances and past behavioral issues. This information can provide helpful pieces to the puzzle. Here are some additional ways you may be able to detect a trauma history:

- Watch to see whether there is a predictable cycle with regard to the student's behavior (see the diagram below). Activation of the body's stress response system begins with a trigger, or something that leads to the student feeling unsafe or emotionally dysregulated. After the student is triggered, there is a period of agitation, which can last for varying amounts of time. Agitation can look like pacing, tapping a pencil, antagonizing others, or any other behavior that demonstrates a feeling of unrest.

- When momentum of the agitation starts to build, the student enters the acceleration phase and completion of the cycle is inevitable. After the student reaches the peak of the stress response, they begin to de-escalate and calm their bodies. As long as the student is not triggered again, de-escalation continues until the student has returned to a recovered state.

- Ask the student to describe the physical sensations they experienced. When the body's stress response is activated, there are certain physical symptoms that you can expect. See the exercise My Body's Response to Stress on the next page to help record the physical sensations.

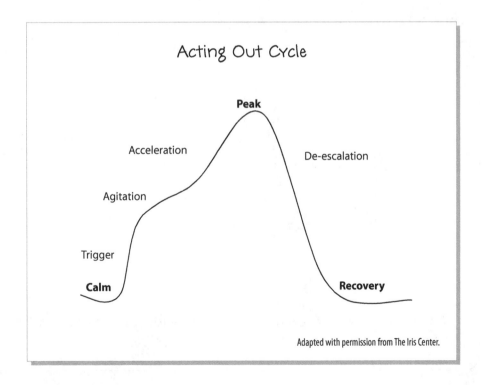

Acting Out Cycle

Peak

Acceleration

De-escalation

Agitation

Trigger

Calm

Recovery

Adapted with permission from The Iris Center.

My Body's Response to Stress

What do you notice in your body when you become angry, frustrated, scared, or overwhelmed? Our bodies give us warning signals that we are becoming stressed. Circle any areas on the body where you can feel your warning signals.

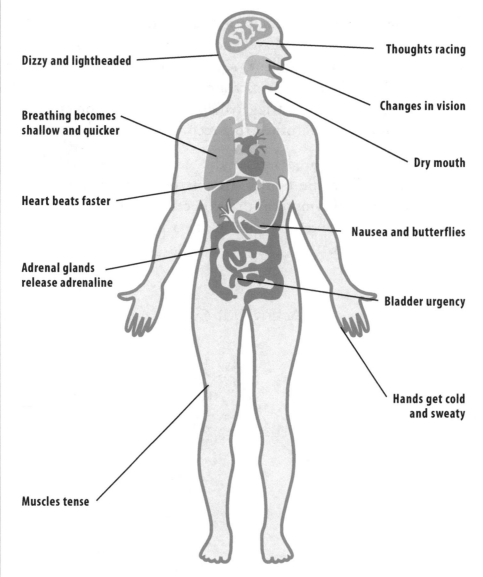

Go over these with a teacher or caregiver and let them know which ones you experience.

The good news is that due to the brain's ability to constantly grow and adapt, there is a lot we can do to help a student become calm and choose an adaptive strategy to self-regulate. I will discuss practical ways to accomplish this in future chapters.

3.

Rebuilding the Structure with New Tools, Skills, and Experiences

Having a sturdy and strong foundation is one of the most important parts of building a house. Similarly, there are certain concepts that you must understand in order to set up a classroom environment that is conducive to learning for all students.

Neuroplasticity

In order to fully understand how you, as an adult in a child's life, can respond in the moment when a child becomes dysregulated and help to rebuild the structure of their brain, you will need to understand the basic concept of neuroplasticity. According to the Oxford Dictionary, *neuroplasticity* is defined as "the ability of the brain to form and reorganize synaptic connections, especially in response to learning or experience." So what does this mean for you as a classroom teacher?

You can have a life-changing impact on students by helping them learn and practice new behaviors and skills that will help them respond adaptively and achieve success academically and socially.

It used to be thought that the IQ and temperament a child was born with was fixed for the remainder of their life. The old school thinking was that if a child experienced a traumatic event or an extended period of abuse, the damage to the child's brain would be permanent. However, the understanding today is much different. None of us are destined to a lifetime of the negative effects of trauma, and our IQs are fluid, changing based on how we use our brains. Essentially, the concept of neuroplasticity should make educators feel hopeful and empowered. You have tremendous potential to help a student overcome the negative effects of trauma, and the following chapters of this book will serve as a guide to help you do just that!

The Importance of Developing Intrinsic Motivation

Traditionally in schools, the discipline and behavior management systems are based on behavioral theory. In the 1950s, B.F. Skinner first described the behavioral approach to human behavior, which was based on the principle of reinforcement (Schacter, 2011). He believed that one's future actions are dependent on the consequences of previous actions. For example, if the consequences are very negative, the likelihood of that behavior being repeated is low; and if the consequences (rewards) are positive, the individual is more likely to act in the same way in the future.

A behavioral approach to discipline and/or classroom management, such as Positive Behavior Intervention and Supports (PBIS) and Classroom Dojo, uses extrinsic rewards and punishments in order to encourage or discourage particular behaviors. However, extrinsically motivating a student to be compliant will only have a short-term, temporary impact, if it has any at all. Therefore, it is very important to also find ways to help students experience intrinsic rewards for their behavior.

For example, when a student studies for a test and earns an A, the feelings of pride, happiness, and satisfaction that the student experiences are intrinsic rewards. True motivation must come from within, and it is 10 times stronger than any extrinsic consequences (Clanton Harpine, 2015). A singular focus on extrinsic consequences actually undermines the development of intrinsic motivation in students.

According to researcher Daniel Pink, intrinsic motivation develops when three conditions are met: (1) the student can experience mastery of the expectation, (2) the student is given some degree of autonomy regarding their learning, and (3) the student understands the purpose of the given expectation and is able to understand the relevance to their own life (Pink, 2009). This concept is extremely important in terms of establishing a learning environment and conditions for learning in which the student feels comfortable and can be successful. When a student experiences mastery, autonomy, and purpose, they become more engaged in the learning process and feel they are a part of the classroom community. This is absolutely essential for a student who has a trauma history.

The next worksheet will guide you through the process of identifying an unmet expectation you have for a student, and how you can foster intrinsic motivation and engagement so that the required skills can be developed. As a result, the student will be able to meet the expectation and begin to develop the intrinsic motivation that will carry over into other tasks.

Fostering Intrinsic Motivation

Name of student: _____

Use this worksheet to plan how you will strengthen intrinsic motivation by factoring in mastery, autonomy, and purpose.

Describe an expectation (behavioral, academic, or social) that the student is not able to consistently meet:

_____

_____

How can you help the student achieve mastery with this expectation? (e.g., break it into smaller segments, provide support, gather resources, teach and practice a particular skill)

_____

_____

How can you incorporate more autonomy into this expectation so that the student has more control of the process?

_____

_____

What is the purpose of this expectation, or why is it important for the student to meet? How does it relate to something that is of importance to the student?

_____

_____

Trauma-Compassionate Responses to Challenging Behavior

Although you need to do the heavy lifting and the majority of the work proactively in order to prevent challenging behavior, teachers are often confronted with a student who has been triggered in some way and is exhibiting challenging behavior. It is important to have a game plan so that you don't get stuck in a situation where you are trying to figure out what to say in the moment, while the entire class is watching. In addition to having a game plan, there are also certain phrases or ways of interacting with a student who has been triggered that will increase the likelihood the situation will be quickly resolved and de-escalated.

When confronted with challenging, aggressive, or even violent behavior, the immediate response is often to ask the student, "What is wrong with you?" However, saying "What has happened to you?" instead is a much less confrontational, accusatory way to approach a student who is in crisis. "What has happened to you?" gives the message that you know the student is having a hard time and that it is because of something that has triggered them. It lets the student know you care enough about them to listen and try to understand what was happening from their perspective. It is an excellent way to begin to build trust and a positive relationship.

Your number one priority when a student is exhibiting challenging behavior is to help them become regulated. Self-regulation is the nervous system's ability to attain, maintain, and change levels of arousal to meet the demands of a given situation. The ability to maintain appropriate levels of arousal develops from our ability to balance (regulate) sensory input from our environment. The challenging behaviors that you see are merely symptoms of dysregulation in your students.

Everyone becomes dysregulated at times (experiencing anger, impatience, fatigue, panic, or boredom) and as adults, most of us have discovered the ways of regulation that work best for us. For example, a person who is experiencing anxiety may choose to go for a run in order to regulate their mind and body. When a child is not yet able to self-regulate, they need external regulation. This is something you can provide by using a calm voice, remaining regulated yourself, and supporting the child in using a strategy that will help them regulate.

Talking about or threatening consequences during an escalated state will only further escalate the situation. The student will perceive it as threatening and cannot use logic or reason while in fight, flight, or freeze mode. Instead, you could set up a resiliency area of the classroom where there are various supports to help students regulate. Think of this as an experiment to determine what works best for each of your students who have experienced trauma. You can use the worksheet that follows to make a plan for each student, and track which strategy is most effective for them.

Type of Sensory Input	Calming Rhythmic and Repetitive	Alerting Arrhythmic and Unpredictable
Vestibular (movement)	✓ Swing ✓ Rolling over a ball ✓ Rocking	✓ Fast, irregular bouncing, spinning ✓ Vibration
Proprioceptive (heavy work)	✓ Joint compressions ✓ Pushing, pulling heavy objects ✓ Climbing, crawling ✓ Jumping	✓ Some children become overstimulated by proprioceptive input
Auditory (sound)	✓ Soft music ✓ Soft singing ✓ Soft voice	✓ Loud music ✓ Fast beat ✓ High amount of verbal input
Tactile (touch)	✓ Wrap in blanket or sleeping bag ✓ Firm touch, massage ✓ Heavy blanket	✓ Light touch, stroking ✓ Cold temperatures ✓ Unpredictable touch

Adapted with permission from www.thinkkids.org

Crisis Plan

Develop a proactive plan that provides guidance regarding how best to deescalate a crisis situation with this student. This worksheet will help you determine the trigger(s), describe the type of stress response and resulting behavior, and track the self-regulation strategies that have been effective.

Student's name: _____

Describe observed behavior: _____

_____

_____

Trigger: _____

Response type: ☐ Fight   ☐ Flight   ☐ Freeze

Strategies tried:

_____

_____

Were the strategies successful?

_____

_____

Describe the process:

_____

_____

_____

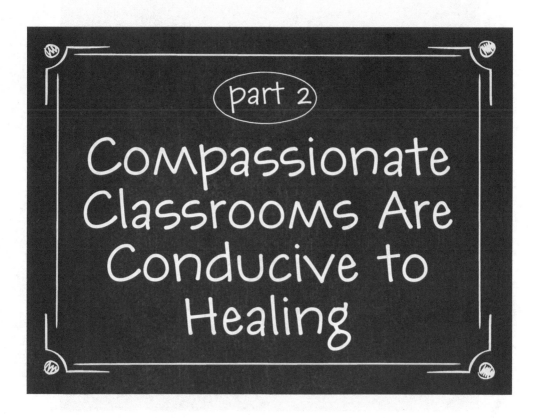

part 2

Compassionate Classrooms Are Conducive to Healing

4.

Building a Solid Structure with a Collaborative Classroom

In my experience, there are four components that, when used in combination, result in a trauma-compassionate classroom in which all students feel safe and are able to learn. A trauma-compassionate classroom is led by a teacher who believes that "kids do well if they can, and if they can't, something is getting in the way. It is up to us, as the adults, to figure out what that is so that we can help" (Greene, 2008). In addition, a trauma-compassionate classroom is collaborative and strengths-based, and in combination, we are able to establish an environment that fosters trust, positive relationships, skill-building, and, ultimately, more successful students.

Your Mindset Determines Your Response

The way you think about a problem will determine how you respond to it. The same is true regarding challenging behavior within your classroom. If you are thinking that a student is not getting started on their writing because they don't care about school and don't feel like putting forth the required effort, you would most likely respond by trying to motivate the student to get started, possibly with some feelings of frustration regarding the amount of time and attention this student requires. In contrast, if instead you asked yourself, "What is it about this expectation that is difficult for them?" you are more likely to respond in a curious, supportive way, with the primary goal of learning more about the student's perspective.

Collaborative Versus Punitive Discipline

According to the work of Dr. Ross Greene, in order to help a student meet an expectation with which they are struggling, a collaborative discussion is an effective, trauma-informed approach (Greene, 2008). A traditional, punitive method of addressing challenging behavior (losing points, name on board, moving clip down, referral, in-school and out-of-school suspension) addresses the behavior on a surface level, and doesn't do anything to change that behavior going forward.

Another unintended outcome of a punitive approach is that through the exertion of power and authority, the student is often left feeling misunderstood and further alienated from school. Therefore, a collaborative approach to discipline is much more effective because it improves the relationship between the adult and the student, and it helps the student build the cognitive skills needed to meet the expectation. In a collaborative discussion, the following conditions must be met:

- Both the adult's and the student's needs are equally important.

- The adult and student both suggest possible solutions to the issue, then evaluate them together. The goal is to decide together on a solution that meets both the adult's and the student's needs.

- The adult is not telling the student how to solve the problem.

Strengths-Based Versus Problem-Focused

Viewing all of your students through a strengths-based lens is another incredibly powerful way to create a trauma-compassionate classroom. This, however, is not typically how the systems in schools are set up. Schools in the United States are very problem-focused, which means that we look for problems with students and then try to solve them. We use things like resource rooms, reading and math specialists, Individualized Education Plans (IEPs), and extended-day programs to infuse struggling students with additional learning time. But in doing so, we are missing a very powerful piece of the puzzle.

When educators (and parents, for that matter) look, first and foremost, for a student's strengths, gifts, talents, and passions, there is much more capacity for growth.

When we recognize and make a concerted effort to focus on and develop strengths, we can teach in a way that will be more effective. Robert Brooks talks about building a student's "islands of competence" as one way to improve resilience (Brooks & Goldstein, 2001). Thomas Armstrong has dedicated his career to showing educators how focusing on a student's strengths increases self-esteem, self-efficacy, and engagement in school (Armstrong, 2012). Richard DuFour, a well-known educator, researcher, and author says it best when he says, "What you see in others depends on what you are looking for" (DuFour, 2002).

Mindful Communication

Children who have experienced trauma are very observant and often hypervigilant. This extreme sensitivity is a mechanism that helped to keep them safe in a traumatic environment. This is important for you to understand because they are also hypervigilant in your classroom. They read your facial expressions when you may not even realize you had one; they are sensitive to the volume and tone of your voice; they can even feel your energy when you haven't even spoken any words.

For these reasons, it is crucial for you to be mindful in your communication. We communicate nonverbally with our posture, facial expressions, proximity, and body language, and for students who have experienced trauma, they are receiving even more of these nonverbal messages. Be aware of your nonverbal communication in your classroom. What might your students be perceiving about your mood, stress level, frustration tolerance, and feelings? Have your student complete the following worksheet, rating how difficult these things are for them on a scale of 1-5, where 1 is not challenging at all and 5 represents very challenging.

Mindful Communication

It is crucial to be mindful in your communication. Complete the questions below, rating how difficult this is on a scale of 1-5, where 1 is not challenging, and five is very hard. Then note what you can do to improve your communication style.

	How Challenging Is This for You?	What Can You Do to Improve in This Area?
Presence: Be fully present in the conversation, actively listen, and do not think about what you will say next while the other person is talking.		
Intention: Enter into the conversation with a curiosity about the other person's point of view, not your agenda or a preconceived notion of the outcome.		
Attention: Shift your attention away from your own needs and desired outcome and focus on what is important to the other person. What do they need from this conversation?		

Restorative Practices

Restorative practices, which emphasize relationship-building and repairing rather than punishing, can play a very important role in building a solid foundation for students with trauma histories. According to the International Institute for Restorative Practices (IIRP), restorative circles have the goal of building community by strengthening or repairing relationships (Costello, Watchel, & Watchel, 2010). Restorative practices evolved from restorative justice, an approach to dealing with criminal offenders by focusing on repairing the harm done rather than on punishment (although punishment, such as incarceration, is sometimes also a consequence).

Restorative circles incorporate many of the principles I have mentioned thus far. They are collaborative, strengths-based, and relationship-building and encourage mindful communication. The premise of restorative circles is that students are more engaged and accepting of guidance when the authority figures such as teachers, administrators, or parents, participate in a problem-solving process with them and for them, as opposed to issuing an edict to them.

In an effort to build a positive classroom community, where every student has a voice, you may choose to begin by starting each week (or each day) with a morning meeting. The following worksheet will serve as a template to help you plan the different aspects of the meeting and how it will flow.

Today's Morning Meeting

Date: _____

Greeting: _____

_____

Sharing about: _____

_____

Group Activity:

Poem   Dancing   Singing

Game   Yoga   Meditation

Other: _____

_____

Morning message: _____

_____

_____

_____

Adapted from www.responsiveclassroom.org

What Does a Collaborative Classroom Look Like?

Just as with restorative practices, in a collaborative classroom, the adult does not serve as an authority figure. Educators are partners in learning and facilitators of problem solving and skill building. The crucial ideas here are that collaboration creates an emotionally-safe environment where all students and their mistakes are accepted and that students are more likely to be engaged in learning and intrinsically motivated. Challenging behavior is addressed by looking at the root cause, then building the skills needed to help the student meet the behavioral expectations.

A collaborative classroom allows a child with a trauma history to thrive. When teachers use punitive discipline (such as referrals, suspension, and losing recess time), behaviorally-based extrinsic motivational programs, or any type of authoritarian approach, the trust between teacher and student erodes and the relationship suffers. A collaborative classroom is empowering, engaging, and empathetic. Here are some things you might notice if you were observing a collaborative classroom:

- Student choice
- Positive interactions, dialogue, and discussions
- Shared responsibility
- Flexibility
- Encouraging risks
- Student-led discussions and activities
- Fostering a discovery-filled environment
- On-task behavior
- Engaged students
- Use of multiple resources
- Positive relationships/reassurance
- "We can" attitude
- Emotionally safe
- Peer collaboration

Qualities of a Collaborative Classroom

You can use this as a guide for what you would like to incorporate in your classroom as you are becoming more collaborative. In addition, there may be some practices or policies that you would like to eliminate from your classroom to increase collaboration.

	What You Will See	**What You Will Not See**
Mindset		
Key Phrases		
Peer Interactions		
Student Engagement		

Classroom Management		
Ways of Demonstrating Learning		
Authority		
Other:		
Other:		

Action steps I will take: _____

_____

_____

_____

_____

_____

When working with students who have experienced trauma, it is common for them to have many behavioral and/or learning challenges present at the same time. As an educator with many students in your classroom, it can be overwhelming to look at each student and their specific issues.

One of the things that I have found to be very effective when coaching teachers is to encourage them to use a laser-like focus on one student and one issue at a time.

Rather than spreading yourself so thin that you don't have the resources to manage any of the issues effectively, prioritizing the student and issue that you want to address first is helpful.

5.

Connection Is the Cement That Builds Sturdy Walls

Research on resilience indicates that all children have the ability to adapt to and overcome adversity when they have the support they need from a caring adult. Educators have a unique and powerful opportunity to provide that support, especially with an understanding of how to form a positive relationship with a student who may be hard to reach.

The next several worksheets provide strategies and tools for fostering relationships with students. As you are giving students the following worksheets, take a moment to reflect on your own teaching style and relationships with students. What can you glean from the very special qualities of your favorite teacher and what can you incorporate into your own teaching style?

My Favorite Teacher EVER

Do you remember your favorite teacher and what an impact this teacher had on your life? Answer the following questions which are intended to help you identify exactly what it was that you loved about this teacher.

1. How did this teacher demonstrate caring and kindness?

   _____

   _____

   _____

   _____

2. How did this teacher share responsibility for your classroom (allow students responsibility and freedom within the classroom)?

   _____

   _____

   _____

   _____

3. How did this teacher demonstrate sensitivity, acceptance, and encouragement toward you? Did this teacher make every child in your classroom feel special?

   _____

   _____

   _____

   _____

4. How did this teacher help you succeed with your learning experiences? Did this teacher provide meaningful learning experiences for every child in your classroom?

_____

_____

_____

_____

5. How did this teacher encourage you to be creative in the classroom?

_____

_____

_____

_____

Getting to Know You Survey

It is important to me to get to know you and to learn what I can do in order to be the best teacher for you. Please answer the following questions so that I can learn more about you.

1. What would be the most useful thing for me to know about you as a student?

   _____

   _____

   _____

2. What do you wish was different about school?

   _____

   _____

   _____

3. Describe a moment in school last year when you felt really engaged. Why do you think that moment was such a positive one for you?

   _____

   _____

   _____

4. What do you think teachers think about you, and what do you wish they'd think about you?

_____

_____

_____

5. Tell me about a teacher who you feel knew you well. What kind of student were you in their class? What did they do to get to know you?

_____

_____

_____

6. If you could build a school, what would it look like?

_____

_____

_____

7. What do you wish I would ask you so that I can be a good teacher for you?

_____

_____

_____

8. What makes a weekend day great for you?

_____

_____

_____

Interest Survey

Learning as much as I can about my students and their interests helps me to be a better teacher. Please complete the following survey about the things you like to read, watch, and do.

1. What kinds of things do you prefer to read? Check all that apply.

   ___ Magazines   ___ Novels (fiction)

   ___ Newspapers   ___ Informational books (nonfiction)

   ___ Poetry   ___ Biographies/autobiographies

   ___ Plays (drama)   ___ Blogs and internet-oriented writing

2. If you like reading fiction, what types of stories (genres) do you prefer? Or, if you're not a reader, what types of movies, TV shows, and video games do you prefer? Check all that apply.

   ___ Adventure/survival   ___ Fantasy

   ___ Mystery/suspense   ___ Science fiction

   ___ Romance/relationships   ___ Horror

   ___ Historical fiction   ___ Graphic novels

   ___ Realistic/reality fiction ___ Humor

   ___ Other, such as _____

3. If you like reading nonfiction, what genres do you prefer? Or, if you're not a reader, what types of movies, TV shows, and video games do you prefer? Check all that apply.

___ True crime	___ Science
___ Health/wellness/fitness	___ Technology
___ Art	___ Biography/autobiography
___ Sports	___ Graphic novels
___ History	___ Religion
___ Politics	___ Music
___ War	___ Other, such as _____

4. When looking for a good book, which of these would you consider? Check all that apply.

___ Friend's recommendation

___ Teacher's recommendation

___ Librarian's recommendation

___ Parent's recommendation

___ Browsing in a bookstore

___ Browsing in the library

___ Looking online

___ Other, such as _____

5. What's the best book you ever read? _____

_____

Why? _____

_____

_____

6. What are your top three favorite . . .

Movies: _____   TV shows: _____

_____   _____

_____   _____

7. In your free time, what things do you most like to do? Give three examples.

1. _____

2. _____

3. _____

Making a plan to repair or strengthen your relationship with a student can be a powerful way to start building the foundation that is required to reduce challenging behavior.

Use the following Relationship Plan worksheet to reflect on the areas of strength and weakness that currently exist in your relationship with a particular student. You may choose to have that student complete this exercise as well. The completed plan can serve as a discussion tool to begin the process of repairing and strengthening your relationship.

Relationship Plan

In an effort to improve our relationship, please answer the following questions about what is working and what you would like to be different.

1. What damage do you need to repair?

_____

_____

_____

_____

2. What do you need to stop doing?

_____

_____

_____

_____

3. What is working in the relationship that you want to continue?

_____

_____

_____

_____

4. What do you need to start doing to improve the relationship?

_____

_____

_____

_____

Connecting with the Family

All students perform their best when schools and caregivers work together as partners. It may be very challenging to form this partnership, especially for children who have experienced trauma and come from homes where parents/caregivers may have had negative school experiences themselves. In cases like this, parents may feel judged or intimidated by teachers, administrators, and the school environment in general.

There are steps that you can take to increase the chances of being able to form a positive partnership with parents. Research indicates that home visits can be extremely effective when done in a proactive, strengths-based manner (Epstein & Salinas, 2004). The following worksheet suggests asking six important questions during a home visit.

Also included in this chapter is a Home/School Collaboration Tool. This worksheet serves as a guidance document to help facilitate discussion and share the perspectives of both the caregivers and the school. The more information you have from the family about their student, the better you will be able to meet their needs in the classroom.

Six Questions to Ask During Home Visits

It can be overwhelming to think of questions to ask families that are both meaningful and unobtrusive. Here is a list of questions from "Lessons at the Kitchen Table" that will provide rich conversations, as well as a template for common procedure for staff. You will notice there are two bullet points with room for questions that you may add.

- What are you most proud of about your son or daughter (granddaughter, niece, sister, etc.)?

- When your child talks about school, what are some of the things they have mentioned?

- In the past, what things at school have made them feel included?

- What gives your family strength?

- What do you think would be particularly important or interesting for them to learn?

- Are there ways in which you, as a parent or caregiver, would like to participate/volunteer at school?

- _____

  _____

- _____

  _____

Home/School Collaboration Tool

You know your child best, and your insights and suggestions are valuable to the school. Please use this form to share information with your child's teacher and other school personnel so that we can collaborate to best meet the needs of your child.

My child's greatest strengths are:

_____

_____

_____

My child is passionate about:

_____

_____

_____

My child struggles with the following skill areas:

☐ Executive function

☐ Emotion regulation

☐ Cognitive flexibility

☐ Language processing

☐ Social skills

Specific expectations at home that my child has had difficulty meeting:

_____

_____

_____

I have identified the following triggers for my child:

_____

_____

_____

Problems that I am solving/have solved at home:

_____

_____

_____

Solutions/strategies I have put in place:

_____

_____

_____

Summary of what has worked well:

_____

_____

_____

6.

Triggers Are Windows to See Beyond the Behavior

A trigger is something that leads to an undesirable reaction or behavior when experienced. For example, one of my biggest triggers is being late to a meeting or event. When I know that I am going to be late to something, I start to notice certain thoughts coming into my mind and a physical response to those thoughts happening in my body. I might have thoughts such as, "People in this meeting will see this as disrespectful of their time" or "I am worried that I will miss something important." Within my body, I start to feel my heart pounding, my face getting hot, and my hands beginning to sweat.

The following worksheets will help you to identify the triggers in your students and how you can provide support to improve behavior.

Identifying Triggers

Triggers are very powerful clues that help us understand how to respond in a way that will be most helpful to the student. This worksheet is designed to help you identify what the particular triggers may be for your student(s).

There is **ALWAYS** a trigger for challenging behavior. What options do you have once you identify the trigger(s)?

_____

_____

_____

Reflecting on your own triggers and how you respond to them can help you identify student triggers. What is one trigger for you that leads to your own undesirable behavior?

_____

_____

Please list some of the triggers for your student that have led to challenging behavior:

_____   _____

_____   _____

_____   _____

What, if anything, can you do to reduce any of the triggers?

_____

_____

Trigger Inventory

Once you determine the student's triggers or trigger areas, you will be able to work with the student to prevent, avoid, or prepare for it. This is an important step in helping the student learn to self-regulate.

Use the following page to describe the feelings or circumstances that tend to set the student off and lead to challenging behavior.

Physical—hunger, fatigue, pain, sickness, hot, cold

Emotional—embarrassed, disappointed, scared, frustrated, sad, excited, lack of connection/relationship

Sensory—loud noise, bright lights, tight clothing, difficulty calming body after being active, texture, taste, crowded spaces

Social—being excluded, being bullied, disagreement with a friend, social media pressures

Academic—work is challenging, doesn't understand what is being taught, pace of class is too fast, forgetting homework, feeling disorganized

Personality—feeling controlled, making a mistake, being lied to, overwhelmed

Daily Routine—being late, transitions

Physical:

_____

_____

Emotional:

_____

_____

Sensory:

_____

_____

Social:

_____

_____

Academic:

_____

_____

Personality:

_____

_____

Daily Routine:

_____

_____

Improving Behavior by Planning for Triggers

Use the table below to gain a better understanding of how to prevent, avoid, prepare for, or provide support regarding the specific triggers for this student. This is something that can be done collaboratively with the student.

Trigger	Prevent *Can you prevent this trigger?*	Avoid *Can you avoid this trigger?*	Prepare *How can you prepare the child to face this trigger?*	Provide Support *How can you support the child so they can be successful?*
1.				
2.				
3.				
4.				
5.				

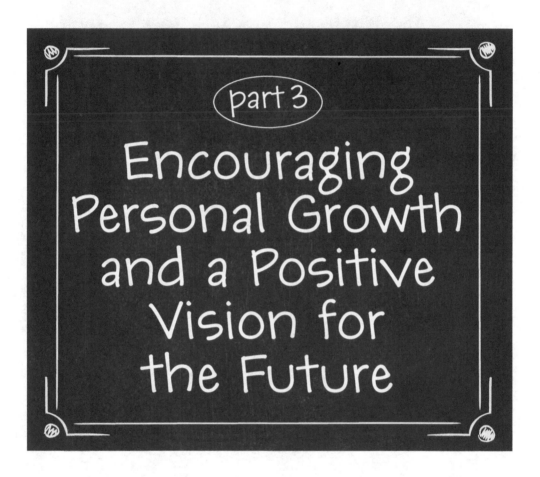

part 3

Encouraging Personal Growth and a Positive Vision for the Future

7.

Resilience Is the Insurance Policy for Future Storms

One of the best ways to promote resilience in students is to come from a glass half-full, strengths-based perspective. When we are problem-focused and looking for deficits we can fix within a student, it negatively impacts self-efficacy and self-esteem, which leads to a lack of engagement and risk-taking.

All of us are born with gifts and talents, and we feel good about ourselves when we have opportunities to showcase them.

This strengths checklist on the following pages can be used to build trust, strengthen relationships, increase self-efficacy and self-esteem, and promote student learning. It can be completed by the student, the teacher, and/or the caregiver, and used to facilitate discussions about the student's interests, passions, gifts, and talents.

You will also find a very powerful Strengths Checklist, developed by Thomas Armstrong, Ph.D., in his book *Neurodiversity in the Classroom*. I find this tool invaluable for really getting to know the student.

Neurodiversity Strengths Checklist

Personal Strengths

_____ Enjoys working independently

_____ Has a good sense of their personal strengths and weaknesses

_____ Learns from past mistakes

_____ Has persistence in carrying out assignments or activities

_____ Is courageous in dealing with adversity or the unknown

_____ Keeps a personal diary or journal

_____ Has a good sense of humor

_____ Possesses a sense of responsibility

_____ Has strong opinions about controversial topics

_____ Marches to the beat of a different drum

_____ Handles stressful events well (is resilient)

_____ Has good character (honesty, integrity, fairness)

_____ Has the ability to set realistic goals

_____ Has a sense of confidence or high self-esteem

_____ Has good self-discipline

_____ Has personal ambitions in life

_____ Displays good common sense

_____ Possesses personal vitality, vigor, or energy

Communication Strengths

_____ Explains ideas or concepts well to others

_____ Asks good questions

_____ Is a good storyteller

_____ Is a good joke teller

_____ Has good listening skills

_____ Handles verbal feedback well

_____ Has good articulation ability

_____ Is able to effectively use nonverbal cues to communicate with others

_____ Is persuasive in getting someone to do something

_____ Has good assertive skills without being pushy

Social Strengths

_____ Has leadership ability

_____ Has a good sense of empathy for others

_____ Enjoys socializing with others

_____ Is good at helping others

_____ Is kind or affectionate toward others

_____ Prefers working with others

_____ Has skills in refereeing disputes between classmates

_____ Is polite and has good manners

_____ Is able to work out their own conflicts with others

_____ Works well in groups

_____ Volunteers their time to a worthy cause

_____ Is good at sharing

_____ Follows class rules

_____ Is liked by their peers

Emotional Strengths

_____ Is emotionally sensitive to perceiving the world around them

_____ Has an optimistic attitude toward life

_____ Can tell how they are feeling at any given moment

_____ Can easily pick up on the emotional state of another person

_____ Is able to handle strong internal feelings in a constructive manner

_____ Receives "gut feelings" about things

Cognitive Strengths

_____ Has good organizational skills

_____ Has good study skills

_____ Is able to use cognitive strategies (self-talk) in solving problems

_____ Is able to pay close attention to details

_____ Has a good short-term or long-term memory

_____ Is able to think ahead

_____ Is able to become totally absorbed in an activity

_____ Can easily divide their attention between two or more activities (multitask)

Creative Strengths

_____ Expresses themselves dramatically

_____ Has a good imagination

_____ Enjoys doodling, drawing, or painting

_____ Likes to act in plays or skits

_____ Demonstrates creativity in one or more school assignments

_____ Possesses a love of beautiful things

_____ Has ideas for futuristic or fantastic projects

_____ Comes up with ideas no one else has thought of

Literacy Strengths

_____ Enjoys reading

_____ Has good reading comprehension

_____ Enjoys doing word puzzles or playing word games

_____ Is a good writer

_____ Is a good speller

_____ Has a large vocabulary

_____ Enjoys listening to audiobooks or to someone telling a story or reading out loud

Logical Strengths

_____ Does well in science class

_____ Can estimate things easily

_____ Enjoys working with numbers/statistics

_____ Is good at solving math problems

_____ Has a chemistry set or other science kit that they work with at home

_____ Has an interest in astronomy, chemistry, physics, or biology

_____ Enjoys logical or number games or puzzles like Rubik's Cube® or sudoku

_____ Can easily calculate numbers in their head

Visual-Spatial Strengths

_____ Has an aptitude for fixing machines

_____ Likes to create three-dimensional structures with building materials

_____ Is good at jigsaw puzzles

_____ Is able to read maps well

_____ Reports being able to visualize images clearly

_____ Is sensitive to the visual world around them

Physical Strengths

_____ Has a good sense of balance

_____ Likes to ride their bike, skateboard, or other self-powered vehicle

_____ Is good at playing team sports

_____ Is good at playing individual sports

_____ Is in good physical health

_____ Likes to dance

_____ Is physically strong

_____ Is a fast runner or has other athletic abilities

_____ Likes to exercise

Dexterity Strengths

_____ Has a hobby building model cars, planes, ships, etc.

_____ Displays good handwriting

_____ Likes to juggle or do magic tricks

_____ Enjoys crafts like knitting

_____ Likes to make things with their hands

_____ Has good tactile ability

_____ Enjoys arts and crafts like origami, collage, or papier-mâché

_____ Enjoys woodworking, carpentry, carving, or metal work

_____ Has good hand-eye coordination

Musical Strengths

_____ Is sensitive to the rhythms of music

_____ Enjoys playing a musical instrument

_____ Knows the music and lyrics of many songs

_____ Has a particular interest in one or more musical genres

_____ Enjoys listening to music

_____ Has a good sense of hearing

_____ Has a good sense of pitch

_____ Has a good singing voice

_____ Makes up their own tunes or melodies with or without lyrics

Nature Strengths

_____ Has a good rapport with animals

_____ Is good at taking care of plants in the classroom or at home

_____ Takes care of a pet at home or at school

_____ Is concerned about the welfare of the planet

_____ Likes to go hiking or camping in nature

_____ Enjoys studying nature

_____ Likes to hunt or fish

High-Tech Strengths

_____ Likes to spend time using a computer or other technology

_____ Has a facility for playing video games

_____ Knows how to set up audiovisual or computer equipment

_____ Enjoys using a still camera or video camera to record events or express themselves

_____ Has several favorite TV shows or movies

_____ Understands at least one computer language

Spiritual Strengths

_____ Enjoys meditation, yoga, or some form of contemplation

_____ Asks big life questions

_____ Has a deep sense of wisdom

_____ Participates in religious or other spiritual events

_____ Has a philosophical attitude toward life

_____ Has a strong faith in something higher than themselves

Cultural Strengths

_____ Has traveled to other countries

_____ Speaks more than one language

_____ Is tolerant of others who have cultural, ethnic, or
racial differences

_____ Has pride in their own cultural, ethnic, or
racial background

_____ Likes to find out about historical events around the world

Other Strengths

_____ Likes collecting things (stamps, coins, buttons, etc.)

_____ Loves to cook

_____ Has a love of learning new things

_____ Is a good test-taker

_____ Possesses a good memory for nighttime dreams

_____ Is curious about the world

_____ Has a good sense of time

_____ Manages money well

_____ Has a good fashion sense

_____ Has good entrepreneurial skills

Reprinted with permission from *Neurodiversity in the Classroom* by Thomas Armstrong, ASCD, 2012.

Action Plan for Showcasing Strengths

Providing opportunities for students to use and develop their strengths promotes social and emotional growth and builds confidence. Use the chart below to find ways for this student to use these strengths throughout the school day.

Strengths	How Can the Student Use This Strength in School?	When/Where?
1.		
2.		
3.		
4.		
5.		

Teaching the Practice of Gratitude

Being grateful for what you have and experiencing the day through a lens of gratitude is one of the most powerful ways a person can experience more joy and happiness.

In his book, *Hardwiring Happiness* (2013), Rick Hanson talks about how practicing gratitude and soaking in positive experiences actually rewire the brain so that, over time, experiencing joy happens more frequently and intuitively. Here are some concrete ways you can teach students to practice gratitude:

- Look for enjoyable moments throughout the day (petting a cat, eating a favorite food, getting a smile from a friend, etc.).

- Remind yourself that there is always someone who is in a worse situation.

- When you become upset or frustrated, quickly state three things for which you are grateful in that moment.

- Say thank you and write thank-you notes to someone who has been kind to you.

- Have a gratitude tree where students can write about things they are grateful for. This can be especially helpful when a student has a negative mindset and would like to shift to a more positive one.

8.

Instilling Hope Is the Promise of Unlimited Potential

The Importance of Hope

Why is hope such an important concept for schools to consider? Over 20 years of research has clearly demonstrated that more hopeful students perform better in school and in life than less hopeful students. Hopeful thought reflects the belief that one can find pathways to desired goals and become motivated to use those pathways. As a result, hope drives the emotions and well-being of people—an essential component of one's happiness and success in life. Hope is positively associated with the following outcomes:

- Self-efficacy and self-worth

- Better attendance

- Optimism

- Higher grades

- Life satisfaction and well-being

- Athletic achievements

- Physical health

- Social competence *(Snyder, Rand, & Sigmon, 2000)*

Although Ruby Payne et al. do not specifically refer to Hope Theory in their book, *Bridges out of Poverty*, central to their observations of families living in poverty is a lack of hope (Payne, DeVol, & Smith, 1999). There is a sense that there is no way out, and they cannot even visualize a life without poverty.

Children who believe they can't meet academic expectations or that education isn't the answer to the problems of poverty are doomed as their beliefs become their reality. However, research in positive psychology suggests that creating hope may be a process we can control versus being an inborn attribute (Sheehan & Rall, 2011). **To have a hopeful school, you must have hopeful teachers because they are the engines driving hope.**

Hope Theory

Charles R. Snyder (1944–2006), a Distinguished Professor of Clinical Psychology at the University of Kansas, developed the field of positive psychology and Hope Theory. His theory of hope consists of three components and was a unique contribution to the field because of his incorporation of the emotions associated with hope. The components are:

1. **Goals**—Hope Theory is based on the assumption that people's actions are goal-directed (Snyder et al., 2000). Goals may be short- or long-term, must be attainable, and almost always contain some degree of uncertainty. Levels of hope are highest when there is a high probability the goal will be attained. Daniel Pink (2009) supports this notion and asserts that mastery of a particular goal or task is motivating. In other words, when we believe we will master a particular task and accomplish a goal, we are motivated to keep working toward it. It is easy to see why it is so important for students to have successes in the classroom. Without experiences of mastery, students will experience very little motivation to persevere.

2. **Pathways Thinking**—This refers to one's belief that they will be able to find a solution to a problem or meet a desired goal. Pathways thinking touches on Albert Bandura's concept of self-

efficacy, or "one's belief in one's ability to succeed in specific situations or accomplish a task" (Bandura, 1994). Bandura (1997) defined four factors that are at the heart of the belief in your own effectiveness (self-efficacy): (1) mastery experiences, (2) vicarious experiences of others, (3) effective persuaders, and (4) a positive social-emotional climate (Sheehan & Rall, 2011). Bandura asserts that self-efficacy is the most important self-reflective ability (Mulhollem, n.d.). It is especially important in schools because students who have high self-efficacy have an increased ability to self-regulate their behavior. Problem solving and critical-thinking skills are important as people generate several alternative solutions to achieve a goal. As barriers present themselves, hopeful people are adept at finding a different way to reach the goal.

3. **Agency Thinking**—This is the motivational component of Hope Theory. Angela Duckworth's research is about the importance of helping students develop perseverance and grit, and that these characteristics have even more to do with achievement than IQ (Duckworth & Seligman, 2005). Hopeful people use self-talk messages such as, "I can do this," and "I am not going to be stopped." When a barrier presents itself, agency thinking (motivation) allows them to put a new plan of action into motion.

As illustrated after setting a goal, pathways thinking (self-efficacy and problem solving) increases agency thinking (motivation and perseverance), which encourages more pathways thinking and agency thinking, which eventually leads to goal attainment. Once a person attains a goal (sense of mastery) it creates the motivation to repeat this cycle.

However, if a person sets a goal and then barriers present themselves, so that they cannot reach that goal, negative emotions result and decrease the feeling of hope. Bandura states that when this process continues over time, people increase self-judgment and those prone to depression treat themselves in a very negative way (Mulhollem, n.d.). An eventual sense of hopelessness results in low self-efficacy, poor motivation, and an unwillingness to take risks because of the possibility of failure.

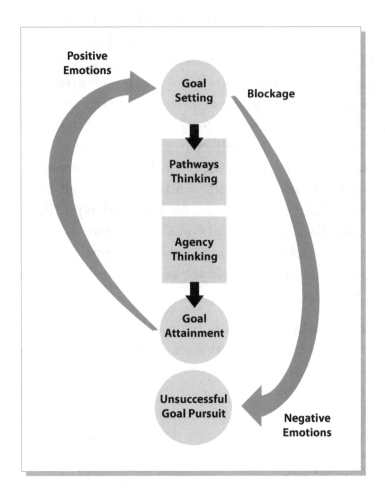

Students must mindfully deal with the powerful and negative emotions that they experience when things go wrong. These negative emotions are natural, and as long as we don't let them control us and paralyze us with fear, they can be very useful in guiding future action.

Strategies for Instilling Hope in Students

Dr. Snyder asserts that as teachers, the most precious commodity we have is the time that we share with our students (1999). This time can take place before school, during or after school, on trips, on weekends, at sporting events, or at clubs. Teachers inadvertently plant seeds of hope by spending large amounts of time with their students.

According to Deborah Mills-Scofield (2012), instilling hope, or the belief that something is possible and probable, should be part of your strategy in the classroom. Some basic principles of using hope as a strategy for student achievement are:

- Base hope on fact, not fiction; hope supports "realistic optimism."

- View failures as learning opportunities.

- Take a strengths perspective and focus on what is working.

- Use optimism as an act of rebellion against the status quo.

Best-Practice School: De La Salle School in Freeport, New York (grades 5–8) is a highly effective school with a 100% high school graduation rate, despite the odds that only one in three students in this community will graduate based on the hardships and adversity they face. Students attribute most of their success to their relationships with their teachers and the school culture built upon Hope Theory. Here are some of the school's best practices:

1. Every morning students recite affirmations such as:

   - I am a leader by choosing to do the right thing even when it means that I am standing alone.

   - I give back to those less fortunate than myself.

   - I dream big.

   - I work hard to achieve my dreams.

2. There are subtle and constant persuaders that all students can achieve the goals they set as a school. These goals are typically things like having good attendance, improved behavior, and passing grades.

3. Goals are reinforced and maintained through weekly award assemblies that recognize goal achievers and celebratory newsletters and posters of award winners are distributed throughout the school.

4. Small class sizes of 15 to 17 students enable teachers to focus more on each student, which allows every student to experience mastery—one of Daniel Pink's three human motivators: mastery, autonomy, and purpose (Pink, 2011).

5. Alumni of the program serve as mentors and living proof of the success that is possible for current students. According to Hope

Theory, alumni are persuaders, sharing their life stories and demonstrating that "others just like you" can achieve these goals.

6. Teachers and students write and share their personal stories of hope and "dream big" visions with the whole school (Sheehan & Rall, 2011).

Additional Hope-Building Strategies

1. **Hope Finding**—The process of making students aware of hope in their own frames of mind as well as in others. The Children's Hope Scale (Snyder et al., 1999) is a simple way to measure hope in students. Teachers can introduce students to the concept of hope through literature. This vicarious learning can teach students the language of hope and highlight how the characters attained hope.

2. **Hope Bonding**—Relationships that serve as persuaders that we will attain our goals and dreams. Every teacher and staff member must serve as persuaders if a school is to create a culture of hope. Teachers must understand the power of their influence to create positive self-beliefs.

3. **Hope Enhancing**—Programs that help students form clear goals, develop pathways to achieve them, summon the energy and will to meet those goals, and possess the ability to reframe obstacles into challenges. The goal here is to get students to buy into their futures. Researchers Susana Marques and Shane Lopez offer these practical strategies for teachers:

Goal Setting

Encourage goals that excite students.

Help students select goals in different life domains and rank them by importance.

Teach students how to set clear markers for goals.

Encourage students to set some "we" goals instead of just "me" goals.

Pathways Thinking

Help students break down goals into smaller subgoals.

Support "keep going" thinking. If one pathway does not work, try others.

Help students recognize if they need a new skill and encourage them to learn it.

Remind students that they can always ask for help.

Agency Thinking

Help students to set "stretch" goals based on past performance.

Help students monitor their self-talk and encourage them to talk in positive voices ("I can do this," and "I will keep at it.").

Tell students stories and provide them with books that portray how other students have succeeded or overcome adversity.

---

4. **Hope Reminding**—Development of a feedback loop allowing students to self-monitor and regulate their hope-enhancing processes. Strategies include use of a hope reminder checklist, reviewing personal help stories, and bonding with people to reinforce hope goals and remove barriers (Sheehan & Rall, 2011).

Humans are wired for hope—we can almost always find a bright spot, even in darkness (McKee, 2008). Given that the development of hope is a process in which teachers can guide students who are currently hopeless to learn to be hopeful, schools have a wonderful opportunity to significantly impact children's lives for the better. The first step is the realization that having hope is an essential component in the foundation of students' educational journeys.

As with any change we are trying to make, a laser-like focus, the concerted effort of all members of the school community, and the use of data to establish a baseline and monitor progress will enable schools to meet the challenge of instilling hope in their young learners. Learning the process and developing the skills to be a more hopeful person are assets your students will carry with them far beyond the school walls. Many students face significant adversity on a daily basis, but instilling hope can empower a lifetime of learning.

Visualizing the Future with "Friendly Wish Poems"

Engaging students in an activity that activates their imaginations and facilitates the process of visualizing a future they would like to live in is one way to have a positive impact for students who have experienced trauma. One way to do this is by having students each write a friendly wish poem. In this exercise, spelling, punctuation, rhythm, and rhyme are not important. The emphasis is on allowing each child's imagination to run free. Here are three examples of wish poems from Susan Kaiser Greenland's book, *The Mindful Child* (2010):

> *I can meet my goals*
>
> *Brave*
>
> *Strong*
>
> *And determined to meet*
>
> *what I need*
>
> *to overcome problems and failures.*
>
> *I wish my life was always peaceful*
> *I wish my life will be successful*
> *I wish my sister will calm down*
> *I wish I will always be safe*
> *I wish my life will be full of excitement.*
>
> *I wish that I can get easy homework*
> *I wish that I can have a lot of animals*
> *I wish that I will never get in trouble.* (pp. 195–196)

9.

Activities That Pave the Road to Success

What Is Mindfulness and How Does It Help?

Mindfulness is paying attention in a particular way, on purpose, to the present moment. Mindfulness can refer to meditation, but you can also practice it during ordinary moments throughout the day. This is a practice that is beneficial for everyone, but it can have many specific benefits for children who have experienced trauma. Challenging behavior by children with a trauma history often has to do with an inability to regulate emotions. The body is often in a state of fight, flight, or freeze due to the steady release of cortisol by the amygdala. When a child experiences trauma over a prolonged period of time, they develop toxic stress, which has a significant impact on learning and behavior.

What really needs to happen is the child needs to feel safe, both physically and emotionally, so that the parasympathetic nervous system can engage and effectively calm the body. All the worksheets and meditations in this chapter are designed to teach the skills required to regulate their emotions.

One of the best ways to help your students develop self-awareness is to teach them how to pay attention to their breath using the Noticing my Breath worksheet on the next page. You can ask them to select one of these times to notice their breath, then have them practice it for the whole week. Each week, they can select a different time to be aware of their breath and continue until they have tried them all.

Noticing My Breath

I Noticed My Breath When...	Days I Noticed My Breath This Week	I Noticed That...
I finished running and/or playing	Monday	
	Tuesday	
	Wednesday	
	Thursday	
	Friday	
	Saturday	
	Sunday	
I was lying in bed at night	Monday	
	Tuesday	
	Wednesday	
	Thursday	
	Friday	
	Saturday	
	Sunday	

I Noticed My Breath When...	Days I Noticed My Breath This Week	I Noticed That...
I was in the shower or bath	Monday Tuesday Wednesday Thursday Friday Saturday Sunday	
I first woke up in the morning	Monday Tuesday Wednesday Thursday Friday Saturday Sunday	

A Radical Act of Kindness

Self-Compassion and Quieting the Inner Voice

Have your students sit comfortably with their eyes closed as you read the following script.

Let's take a few moments to notice what is happening in your body. Notice how it feels to sit in your seat at your desk right now.

Our goal right now is to take good care of ourselves. If thoughts come to mind as you scan the different parts of your body, try not to get caught up in them. Instead, return to noticing how your feet feel as they rest on the floor, and how your hands feel as they rest in your lap.

Try not to analyze or judge anything right now—you are just a friendly and impartial spectator. If you hear a voice in your mind that is being critical or judgmental, that's perfectly natural, just see if you can ignore it by bringing your attention back to your body. You can even whisper silently to yourself, "Not now."

There is no place you have to go right now. There is nothing you need to do. There is no one for you to please. There's no one else you have to be. You don't need anything other than what you have right here. All we are doing now is resting—nothing more and nothing less.

As you feel your body sitting in your chair, imagine that you can see the tension in your body; that your tension is like a gray cloud of smoke. And feel it all leaving your body with each exhale of your breath. Then imagine your tension sinking into the earth below the floor. Now try it again.

Now that all the tension in your body has released into the earth, picture your own safe place. Your safe place can be someplace you've been, someplace you'd like to visit, or an imaginary place. Your safe place is somewhere you feel happy and loved, you are strong and relaxed, and you have lots of fun. Picture yourself having fun and relaxing in your safe place.

Rest in your safe place knowing that you are complete and whole just as you are. You don't need to do anything, you don't need to change, and you don't need to please anyone. A lot of us spend a whole lot of time paying attention to other people. We wonder how others feel, what they think, what they would like us to do, and how they would like us to be.

Right now we are going to give ourselves a break from all the inner talk about what other people think, say, do, and feel. We are going to let go of any thoughts we have about other people right now. We are going to take good care of ourselves and rest.

There is no place you have to go right now. There is nothing you need to do. There is no one for you to please. There's no one else you have to be. You don't need anything other than what you have right here. All we are doing now is resting—nothing more and nothing less.

We are going to end by sending friendly wishes to ourselves. Picture yourself in your safe place where you are laughing and having fun. May you be healthy and strong. May you be with people you love and who love you. Everyone in your safe place is relaxed and at ease. Everyone in your safe place is peaceful and having fun.

Adapted from *The Mindful Child* by Susan Kaiser Greenland, 2010 (p. 122).

Shining a Light on Dark Emotions

When feelings are very intense, there is often an urge to suppress them out of fear. Children who have experienced trauma certainly have many uncomfortable, and maybe even scary, emotions within them. The suppression of these dark emotions often leads to explosions and an inability to regulate one's mood. As a result, challenging behavior often ensues and gets in the way of the learning process for the child, and also for the other students in the classroom.

Once they complete the chart, encourage students to draw a picture of the emotion they are describing.

Recognizing what one is feeling and labeling that emotion can be a challenge for adults and students alike. Using the Labeling Feelings wheel on the next page, begin by having the student identify which of the seven primary emotions in the innermost ring of the circle they are feeling. Move out to the second ring and help the student identify a more specific feeling, and eventually use the outermost ring to become even more specific about the feeling.

Once the student determines the feeling they are experiencing, you can help them work through the chart on the following page to deepen their understanding of their own emotions.

Labeling Feelings

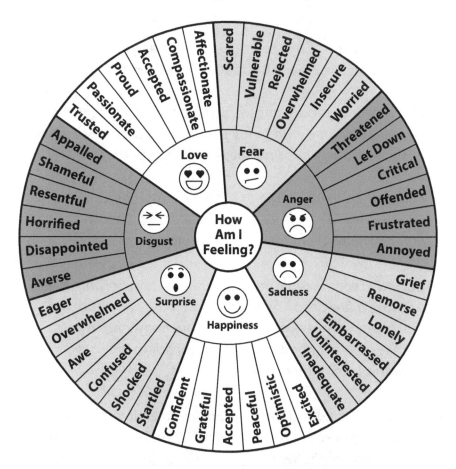

Describe the Situation	What Were You Feeling?	What Did You Feel in Your Body?

Feeling Your Strong Feelings

Read the following script to your students as you guide them in this meditation. You may choose to close your eyes.

Everyone has strong, uncomfortable feelings that surface from time to time, and many people deny these feelings or push them away because they are scared of them.

Rather than being afraid of these feelings, you can turn toward them with curiosity and acceptance, which actually helps them to pass more quickly.

Get into a comfortable position, either sitting or lying down, and take a few deep breaths. As you breathe in, notice the sensations of the oxygen entering your body, and as you exhale, relax your body. Allow your breath to fall back into its natural pace and rhythm.

During this meditation, simply be curious about what is happening in your body and mind. Whatever is happening is okay. Notice the sensations in your body and become aware of your mood. Are you feeling relaxed or tense? Just notice what is happening right now in this moment.

If you are feeling stressed or anxious, remind yourself that it is okay to feel this way. It feels uncomfortable, but it is something you are learning to be more aware of.

Take your time and just notice what is going on. Where is the sensation the strongest? What part of your body feels the weakest sensation?

When we are curious about a challenging experience, we can feel a shift in our attitude and our relationship to what is happening. It is not the situation that makes us upset, it is the way that we are thinking about it and, therefore, how we are choosing to respond that makes us upset.

Our resistance to our negative emotions causes them to grow stronger. When you examine them with curiosity, you are shining a light in the darkest corners of yourself, which actually helps these emotions leave you more quickly.

Take a few more breaths to pay attention to what is happening in your body and mind. When you feel ready, you may open your eyes.

Adapted from *10% Happier* by Dan Harris, 2014.

Creating a Space for Choice

By teaching children how to meditate, then practicing with them regularly, you are helping them develop the skills of attention, focus, self-awareness, and emotional regulation, among other things. Practicing mindfulness is like building a muscle in the gym or improving one's skills in a particular sport. The brain becomes better at noticing when it has been triggered, and recognizing what the fight, flight, or freeze response feels like in the body.

As soon as the child recognizes that they have been triggered, they can shift their focus away from the thoughts that are upsetting them, and onto following their breath. **The ability to shift attention in this way creates a space, or a pause, during which the student can choose how they want to respond to the situation.** The child may self-soothe by saying something like, "I am feeling very upset right now. I know this feeling will pass. I will just focus on my breath while I wait for my body to feel better."

Without this skill, a child who has been triggered will become hijacked by the release of the stress hormone, cortisol, which the amygdala then floods the body with. Once this happens, the child loses the ability to access their prefrontal cortex, the part of the brain responsible for reason, and the only thing to do is wait for the child to calm down.

Providing students with opportunities to practice different calming activities and determine what is most effective, is empowering and skill-building. The following two worksheets can be used to track the strategies and the effectiveness of each. In the end, the student will be able to use these worksheets as a reminder of the tools they can choose to use when upset or dysregulated.

Compassion for Yourself

Guide your students through this mediation script to help them develop compassion towards themselves.

Think about times you have felt cared about by people, pets, or spiritual beings, in your life today or in the past. Any kind of caring for you counts, such as times you were included, seen, appreciated, liked, or even loved.

Relax and open yourself to feeling cared about. If you get distracted, come back to feeling cared about. Stay with these feelings and sense them sinking in, like water into a sponge.

Then think about one or more people you have compassion for—perhaps a friend who is sad, a neighbor who is sick, or refugees on the other side of the world who may not have enough to eat.

Get a sense of their burdens, worries, and suffering. Feel a warmheartedness, a sympathetic concern.

You could have thoughts such as:
*   "May your pain ease."*
*   "May you find work."*
*   "May you get through this illness."*

Give yourself over to compassion, letting it fill you and flow through you.

Now that you know what compassion feels like, apply it

to yourself. Recognize any ways that you feel stressed, tired, ill, mistreated, or unhappy.

Then bring compassion to yourself as you would to a friend who felt like you do. Know that everyone suffers and that you are not alone in your pain. You could have thoughts such as:

> *"May I not suffer."*
> *"May these hurt feelings pass."*
> *"May I not worry so much."*
> *"May I heal from this illness."*

Imagine compassion like a warm rain coming down over you.

Reprinted with permission from *Resilient* by Rick and Forrest Hanson, 2018.

My Personal Calming Strategies

Use the following chart to keep track of the calming strategies that you have tried, and which ones work the best for you. This chart will be a reminder about what you can do to calm yourself down and get back to feeling good.

Trigger	What I Notice in My Body	My Calming Strategies
1.		1. 2. 3.
2.		1. 2. 3.
3.		1. 2. 3.
4.		1. 2. 3.
5.		1. 2. 3.

Empowerment Through Self-Soothing

The ability to calm yourself, or self-soothe, is an extremely important part of the healing process for a child who has experienced trauma. It takes practice, and will look different for each child. The goal is to help the child experiment with different phrases and mantras so they can determine what works best for them. The empowerment lies in the fact that the child is learning they have everything they need, right within them, in order to feel safe and calm.

Mantras are very powerful in re-programming the brain to think different thoughts. The following worksheet can be used by students to keep track of the mantras that are the most meaningful to them. The completed worksheet can serve as a reminder of their favorite mantras.

My Personal Mantras

The things that your inner voice is saying to you day in and day out are affecting the way you feel about yourself and the way you experience the world. Taking charge of what you are saying to yourself by creating some meaningful mantras and practicing them is a powerful way to reprogram your thinking. Use the prompts below to create a few mantras that will be helpful to you when you are feeling down.

When I am feeling sad, it helps to say to myself:

_____

_____

_____

_____

When I am feeling angry, it helps to say to myself:

_____

_____

_____

_____

When I am feeling worried, it helps to say to myself:

_____

_____

_____

_____

When I am feeling scared, it helps to say to myself:

_____

_____

_____

_____

When I am feeling _____, it helps to say to myself:

_____

_____

_____

_____

10.

Final Thoughts

Trauma exists in the lives of many children, and the effects weigh heavily on them. What works for teaching some children will not work for other students, and teachers are not taught in school about mental health and trauma. The clinical treatment of trauma by a social worker or psychologist is helpful, but for many, is not an option. This means that educators are left with the responsibility of knowing what to do and how to best teach these children.

The clinical setting is obviously different from the classroom setting in that the approaches must be tailored. It is my intention that the resources contained within this book will serve that purpose.

As an educator today, a lot is expected of you. Anxiety and depression among children are at an all-time high in this country, and what is required of teachers is more than what has ever been expected. But you have the most important job on this earth, aside from being a parent. Being a teacher is, in my opinion, the highest honor.

We need to properly equip our teachers so they feel competent and have the resources and support to be effective with all students. I hope that the practical knowledge, tools, strategies, and resources within this book will empower you to have confidence that you can meet any challenge that comes your way and will bring you hope that you really can make a difference!

Recommended Resources

Mindfulness Products

Hoberman Sphere

Mind Jar - www.jenniferbashant.com/resources

Mindful Arts Activity Cards - www.mindfulartssf.org/breathing-cards

Mindful Games, Susan Kaiser Greenland

Mindfulness Cards for Teens, Gina M. Biegel

Rain Stick

Tibetan Singing Bowl

Mindfulness Apps

Buddhify
Buddhify is an interactive app designed to introduce users to techniques of urban meditation, thereby fostering a state of mindfulness and well-being in everyday life situations. The app defines mindfulness as focused awareness of the user's current experience.

Calm®
Calm's mission is to make the world happier and healthier. Calm is a meditation, sleep, and relaxation app, available for all devices.

GoNoodle®
GoNoodle is a series of web-based videos, games, and activities focused on introducing short bursts of physical exercise in the classroom. It helps teachers and parents get kids moving with short interactive activities. Desk-side movement helps kids achieve more by keeping them engaged and motivated throughout the day.

Headspace®
Headspace's goal is to make meditation accessible to everyone. It does this through a smartphone app full of "guided meditations"— audio sessions where one of the company's co-creators leads listeners on a journey of contemplation.

Insight Timer®

Insight Timer is a smartphone app and online community for meditation. The app features guided meditations, music, and talks posted by contributing experts.

Books

Dan Harris: *10% Happier: How I Tamed the Voice in My Head, Reduced Stress Without Losing My Edge, and Found Self-Help That Actually Works – A True Story.*

Daniel Pink: *Drive: The Surprising Truth About What Motivates Us.*

Patricia Jennings: *Mindfulness for Teachers: Simple Skills for Peace and Productivity in the Classroom.*

Rick Hansen: *Hardwiring Happiness: The New Brain Science of Contentment, Calm and Confidence.*

Ross Greene: *Lost at School: Why Our Kids with Behavioral Challenges are Falling Through the Cracks and How We Can Help Them.*

YouTube Videos

Brene Brown: Sympathy Versus Empathy: https://www.youtube.com/watch?v=1Evwgu369Jw

Dan Harris: Why Mindfulness is a Superpower: https://www.youtube.com/watch?v=w6T02g5hnT4

Daniel Pink: Drive Animation: https://www.youtube.com/watch?v=_BmHdTC36N4

Neuroplasticity: https://www.youtube.com/watch?v=ELpfYCZa87g

Rita Pierson: Every Kid Needs a Champion: https://www.youtube.com/watch?v=SFnMTHhKdkw

Harvard Center for the Developing Child: Toxic Stress: https://www.youtube.com/watch?v=rVwFkcOZHJw

References

For your convenience, worksheets and activities are available for download at www.pesi.com/bashant

Armstrong, Thomas. (2012). *Neurodiversity in the classroom: Strength-based strategies to help students with special needs succeed in school and life.* ACSD.

Bandura, A. (1997). *Self-efficacy: The Exercise of Control.* W.H. Freeman and Company.

Bandura, Albert. (1994). Self-efficacy. In V. S. Ramachaudran (Ed.), *Encyclopedia of human behavior,* 4 (pp. 71–81). Academic Press.

Brooks, Robert, & Goldstein, Sam. (2003). *Nurturing resilience in our children: Answers to the most important parenting questions.* Contemporary Books.

Brooks, Robert, & Goldstein, Sam. (2001). *Raising resilient children: Fostering strength, hope and optimism in your child.* Contemporary Books.

Center for Responsive Schools, Inc. (2016). The Joyful Classroom: Practical Ways to Engage and Challenge Students K-6.

Clanton Harpine, E. (2015). Is intrinsic motivation better than extrinsic motivation? In *Group-centered prevention in mental health.* Springer.

Costello, Bob, Wachtel, Joshua, & Wachtel, Ted. (2010). *Restorative circles in schools: Building community and enhancing learning, a practical guide for educators.* International Institute for Restorative Practices.

Duckworth, Angela L., & Seligman, Martin E. P. (2005). Self-discipline outdoes IQ in predicting academic performance of adolescents. *Psychological Science, 16*(12), 939–949.

DuFour, Richard. (2002). *How to develop a professional learning community: Passion and persistence.* [DVD]. Solution Tree Press.

Epstein, Joyce L., & Salinas, Karen Clark, (2004). Partnering with parents and communities. *Education Leadership, 61*(8), 12–18.

Felitti, V. J., Anda, R. F., Nordenberg, D., Williamson, D. F., Spitz, A. M., Edwards, V., Koss, M. P., & Marks, J. S. (1998). The Adverse Childhood Experiences (ACE) Study: Relationship of childhood abuse and household dysfunction to many of the leading causes of death in adults. *American Journal of Preventive Medicine, 14*(4), 245–258.

Greene, Ross W. (2008). *Lost at school: Why our kids with behavioral challenges are falling through the cracks and how we can help them.* Scribner.

Greenland, Susan Kaiser. (2010). *The mindful child: How to help your kid manage stress and become happier, kinder, and more compassionate.* Atria Paperback.

Hanson, Rick. (2013). *Hardwiring happiness: The new science of contentment, calm and confidence.* Harmony Books.

Hanson, Rick, & Hanson, Forrest. (2018). *Resilient: How to grow an unshakable core of calm, strength and happiness.* Harmony Books.

Harris, Dan. (2014). *10% happier: How I tamed the voice in my head, reduced stress without losing my edge, and found self-help that actually works.* IT Books.

Iris Center. (2020). *The acting-out cycle.* Vanderbilt University. https://iris.peabody.vanderbilt.edu/module/bi1/cresource/q2/p02/

Marques, Susana C., Lopez, Shayne J., & Pais-Ribeiro, J. L. (2011). Building hope for the future: A program to foster strengths in middle-school students. *Journal of Happiness Studies, 12*, 139–152.

Marques, Susana C., & Lopez, Shane J. (n.d.). Research-based practice: Building hope in our children. *NASP Communique.*

McKee, Annie. (2008, October 27). Doing the hard work of hope. *Harvard Business Review.*

Mills-Scofield, Deborah. (2012, October 9). Hope is a strategy (well, sort of). *Harvard Business Review.*

Mulhollem, Rodney L. (2009). *A general overview of Bandura's social cognitive theory.* Liberty University.

Payne, R. K., DeVol, P. E., & Smith, T. D. (2006). *Bridges out of poverty: Strategies for professionals and communities.* Highlands, TX: Aha! Process, Inc.

Phifer, Lisa Weed, Crowder, Amanda K., Elsenraat, Tracy, & Hull, Robert. (2017). *CBT toolbox for children & adolescents: Over 200 worksheets & exercises for trauma, ADHD, autism, anxiety, depression & conduct disorders.* PESI Publishing and Media.

Pink, Daniel. (2009). *Drive: The surprising truth about what motivates us.* Riverhead Books.

Schacter, Daniel. (2011). *Psychology* (2nd ed.). Worth Publishers.

Sheehan, Kevin, & Rall, Kevin. (2011). Rediscovering hope: Building school cultures of hope for children of poverty. *Phi Delta Kappan, 93*(3), 44–47.

Snyder, C. R., Rand, Kevin L., & Sigmon, David R. (1999). Hope theory. In C. R. Snyder (Ed.), *Coping: The psychology of what works.* Oxford University Press.

Think Kids. (2019). Massachusetts General Hospital. www.thinkkids.org